To All My Sisters In The Struggle 2ND Edition
Natalie M. Lewis

To All My Sisters in the Struggle 2ND Edition
Author: Natalie M. Lewis
Developmental Editor: Barbara J. King
Copyright 2008©
ISBN 978-0-557-32856-7

All rights reserved. No part of this publication may be reproduced or transmitted in any form or by any means, electronic or mechanical, including photocopy, recording, or any information storage and retrieval system, without the express written permission of the publisher.

Requests for permission to make copies of any part of the work should be emailed to: Permissions Department
Natalie@nataliemlewis.com

My Thanks

I would like to thank my ex-boyfriend for not listening to me when I, disheartenly, asked him to take my life. Also, I would like to thank my Creator, Yahweh, for not allowing me to come home to Heaven when I asked His permission.

I would like to thank everyone in my life, who contributed to my low self-esteem that made me feel unworthy of being one of God's leading ladies.

Through that pain, my purpose came!

I thank you sincerely!

TO ALL MY SISTERS IN THE STRUGGLE

Introduction

This book seeks to rip the bandage off of your wound, off of your sores that are festered with pus from destructive behaviors, thoughts, people and erroneous reasoning in your life. Even though the bandage hurts while it is coming off, it comes off quickly. The injury is not fully healed, and so it may sting a little. It is not totally healed because the bandage has done its job in protecting your laceration from the rest of the elements and the debris that would cause it to become more infected. However, the bandage does its job so well that the wound stays fresh, it stays soft, moist, and in some cases very icky.

I seek to get to that icky part; whether it be physical, social, spiritual, mental, or financial. I seek to allow it to dry out so it can truly form a healthy scab, and help your body return to its, natural, healthy status as God has intended it to be.

Sisters, let the healing begin!

TO ALL MY SISTERS IN THE STRUGGLE

TABLE OF CONTENTS
Introduction 5
The Pawns 9
Suicidal 17
Sexually Dysfunctional 21
Older Does Not Necessarily Mean Wiser 30
The Good Working 33
Never Rationalize Your Discernment 38
How to Fight Back 42
       Round One 44
       Second and Final Round 47
Happy/ Healthy 52
This Is My Story 59
       First 73
       Second 75
Staying Healed 80
       Physical 80
       Social 81
       Spiritual 82
       Mental 83
       Financial 84
Don't Look Back 89

TO ALL MY SISTERS IN THE STRUGGLE

Chapter 1

THE PAWNS

The Enemy started his mission of destroying my faith and love in God from the womb. I was rejected constantly it seemed, by everyone and everything. Some who contributed to the rejection may not even be aware of it. You see, it takes the Enemy, your Adversary, to distort the truth of what is actually being said and to make one perceive it as something harmful enough to postpone or stop your destiny.

I remember being called "Fat Nat" by my siblings, "Ugly" by my classmates, "Big Nose", "Gap-Toothed", and when I started to wear glasses… the infamous "Four Eyes." This feeling of rejection began to manifest not only in the form of those mocking names by my older sisters, but it became more hurtful from the opposite sex. To make matters worse, as I grew to the age of noticing them, a new form of rejection began. If I saw a boy in class that I thought was cute, I would tell a friend. Unfortunately, that so-called friend would tell the boy, and I got horrible results. That cute boy would laugh about it to his friends, and the ridiculing began. Low self-esteem clearly began to develop in me during this time period.

I recall one event in kindergarten when it was about the first day of spring. I wanted to wear shorts to school, and of course, my mom said not to wear them. I decided I would sneak and wear them anyway. Now, remember I was only in kindergarten! I remember the cute pink ruffled shorts that I'd put on under my pants. One of my friends had conspired with me to show off our spring gear. We changed clothes in the bathroom right before Story-time. Oh, I was so excited! As we were sitting there waiting for our teacher to read to us, a boy in my class whispered something about my shorts to the other boys. They laughed because they'd assumed that the shorts were my underwear. That was so embarrassing to say the least. Here I was, trying to impress my classmates, and I got made fun of for wearing what seemed to be panties to class! I wanted to put my pants back on, but I didn't want to let them know that they'd gotten to me, so I didn't.

Another time, I recall wearing my favorite blue zippered, short sleeve top to school. It had a pocket on the chest that zipped up, too. Oh, I loved that shirt. I proudly went to school and showed it to a boy in my class that I liked. I said, "Hey look at my shirt, it zips up and down." His friend sat on the floor with us for Story-time. He told my crush to unzip my top, but make sure he doesn't zip it down far enough to show my "boobies." Embarrassment struck again! I was frozen solid. So, I let my crush unzip my top as I tried to pull away. I think I made enough of an effort to make him feel uncomfortable enough to stop. This rejection from boys and my family, during these formative years of my life, seemed to be the beginning of my not getting the positive results that I sought. Instead, I received negative responses from people who I loved and cared for, ones that I could never have imagined would've treated me that way. I decided to do a better job at impressing a guy the next time. I'd learn how to get their attention, and how to get the response I was desperately seeking.

During this time, the only love I was receiving without question, as I recall, was from my mother. She was my best friend; we did everything together, it seems. I guess because I was the youngest and she didn't work, I had the opportunity to be with her all day long. This was before I began attending Head Start. My father was usually away at work. I remember seeing him occasionally, maybe on the weekends. He spent time with us when he wasn't working, and it was lovely. Now, that's all I remember about my early relationship with my parents.

After Head Start, rejection increased. My family and I were uprooted from Clarksville to Memphis, Tennessee for reasons which we still are not fully aware of today. We only know that my father heard from the Lord and moved out on faith. We moved immediately from Clarksville to Memphis and had to stay with my grandmother. I am sure that my parents felt we would be well taken care of by their immediate family. Unfortunately, this was not the case. I was teased constantly by my aunts and uncles. The same mean names I gave you earlier continued and intensified, because I no longer had my mother around 24/7 to soften the blows of those harsh words. My mother and father were always out looking for work, which left me in the clutches of my relatives who we'd moved in with. My sisters and I were made to do awful things just for my aunt's own enjoyment.

My new school consisted of all black peers with crab-like mentalities. Second grade proved to be worst than Head Start and Kindergarten. I was called everything but a child of God at school. I couldn't concentrate on my schoolwork; I was unprepared because we'd moved so quickly, all my school supplies were at my previous school in Clarksville, TN. On top of all of that, my only brother (my dog Golden) had been hit by a train in my grandparents' back yard. Since no one at school liked me, I went from being extremely talkative to extremely quiet. I had one friend, Andrea; she was nice to me and gave me a pencil on my first day of school. Around the second semester of school, a few other girls in the class warmed up to me, but the guys and stuck-up girls, made continual cruel jokes and comments that would damage my relationships with people for the next 15 years.

As I reflect on these things, I don't hold anything against those students; they didn't know any better, they were just **pawns** in the Enemy's wide scheme of things. They were just a means to an end; a way for the Enemy to convince me that I did not belong, or need to be on planet Earth.

Eventually, I found another crush, Bobby, the cutest little chocolate-skinned boy I'd ever seen! Of course, I would never tell him how I felt; I wasn't up for another round of humiliation that soon. But some way, he found out, and he was nice about it. It seemed to be okay. I felt human again! I thought, "I have a boyfriend woo-hoo!" I became so talkative to the point of getting a spanking in class. I was embarrassed that this happened in front of my new boyfriend; therefore, I broke off our relationship.

I don't know why, but for some reason after that, I always seemed to attract the unattractive boys. One time a guy chased me around the classroom for a kiss. I did not like him, and I was forced to punch him to get away. He reported it to my teacher, who explained to him that's what he deserved.

As time passed, I continued to attract the undesirable boys, you know, the ones no one else wanted, and finally, I gave in to them. Ultimately, I felt it was better to have some love than none at all. In hindsight, I think, subconsciously, I began dating them because I felt that no one would make fun of me. This way, they wouldn't tell the guys that I was too ugly to be with them. On one occasion, a jealous girl did tell my boyfriend, "You could be with me, I look better than her." He agreed and left me for her. This type of thing also happened within my family from elementary to middle school. When I finally did get a boyfriend who was my type, once he looked at my sisters, I was non-existent. The guy would follow behind them like a whining puppy dog! My sisters thought it was so cute to have some little kid liking them, but I didn't. For me, this was more rejection, more pain, and more heartache that grew while the Enemy was sitting back rejoicing. He was definitely watching his master plan for me come into fruition. I began to seek out unattractive guys to date; ones who I knew wouldn't have a chance with my sisters or anyone else prettier than me.

Yes, I continued to lower my qualifications and expectations of the guys I wanted to date.

My new plan was to start from scratch. I would allow unworthy thugs in my life. After that, I would groom them to be worthy of my love. Then, maybe they would appreciate me, never want to leave me, and we would live happily ever after. Again, my desire of achieving love and appreciation from the opposite sex resurfaces here.

The next troubling relationship I recall having, after my elementary days, was in middle school. The problem was that the guy was so nice, too nice, in fact. By this time I was used to being hurt, used to making guys like me unworthily, and I was used to fighting for their love. But with him, I didn't have to do that. One day he called and offered to take me to a Step show. I'd never heard of that type of show before now. After he explained what it was, immediately, I refused. Other than the fact that I was scared at what would happen between us, I knew my parents wouldn't allow me to go. It seemed they were strictly against outings, especially with a so-called "boyfriend" when I was only in the seventh grade. We continued to date, oddly, he'd carried my books without me asking him to; no one had ever done that for me before! Based on what my parents had taught me, I knew that I deserved this type of treatment, but to actually have a nice guy to do it, now that was strange. It was so unusual, that I broke up with him the following week!

Now, as I reflect on that particular relationship, I understand fully why I broke up with him. I guess I remembered how the roughneck type guys would drop their hard acts for my sisters because of their grace and attitude. I wanted to create the same type of experience for me, so that's why I chose the rough guys, in hope of making them worthy of my love, like what I had been taught; like what I'd seen take place between roughneck guys and my other sisters.

I finally came to the realization that I am not my sisters. I want you to have this revelation, as well. God knew what I needed, and He knew what I could tolerate. But because of my desire to be as good as my sisters, and prove to everyone else in my family and school that I was worthy, I took it upon myself to try to create a man who would treat me in a special way. Of course, hindsight is 20/20. That guy who I dated for one week in middle school was really sweet, a perfect gentleman, the type I am waiting for now. I wish I could find him to apologize for what I did to him. I pray he is somewhere still as gentle hearted as he was then, still showing women the royalty they deserve. And I pray that someone is treating him as the king that God has made him to be.

TO ALL MY SISTERS IN THE STRUGGLE

Chapter 2

SUICIDAL

Because of many frustrations in my young life, I didn't want to live anymore. Nothing seemed to work out as I had planned. I wanted love but did not receive the kind of love that I sought after; that I'd prayed for, and worked extremely hard to obtain.

Suicidal thoughts began to fill my mind. At the tender age of ten, I felt like dying. I allowed those thoughts to invade my life and overtake me. I became **suicidal**. I can remember sitting on the floor of our shotgun house, in my room that I shared with my sister, crying because I didn't have any friends. I couldn't go anywhere because of my strict, religious upbringing, and no guy liked me at that time. I was a wreck and couldn't get rid of negative thoughts that kept flooding my mind!

Now remember, I was only 10 years old! A child should have happy memories and experiences; I had no business feeling that way. But the Devil, the Enemy, the Adversary was still working his deceitful plan to ruin and steal my life.

While at home, alone in a room with my sister, I remember sitting on the floor crying. I found a large bottle of aspirin. I remember thinking, "take them all and just die." All of my pain and disappointments would be over. I wouldn't have to be subjected to anymore rejection. This seemed to be the appropriate answer to my immediate problem. This was the perfect solution, or so I thought with my young mind. I wasn't being dramatic. I really wanted to die! I know now that these were not my thoughts - they were whispered in my ear by the Enemy.

I now understand that the Enemy sent the *Spirit of Heaviness*[1] to whisper these thoughts and cause me to want to take my life. He hit me with everything in his arsenal. These are the emotions I experienced:
- Sorrow/Grief
- Insomnia
- Broken Heart
- Self-Pity
- Rejection
- Depression
- Despair
- Hopelessness
- Withdrawal/Pouting
- Excessive Fatigue and Weariness
- Suicidal Thoughts
- Torn Spirit
- Heaviness
- Escape/Indifference
- Bitterness
- Sadness/Abandonment/Loneliness
- Suppressed Emotions
- Physical Illnesses and Pains

---

[1] Isaiah 61:3

Do any of these sound familiar to you? If so, you may be dealing with the *Spirit of Heaviness*. But don't worry, I will tell you how to overcome it in the next few chapters.

My sister is my hero. It is because she was persistent and persuasive in talking me out of ending my own life, that I am able to share my journey with you. I had already taken about four pills. She questioned me about my friends, about what they'd think and feel if I cut my life short. Little did she know, the problem was caused by my friends. I began to cry hysterically. She asked me about how I thought my parents would feel if I took my life. My response to her was, "They still have three other girls." She then said something that made me put down the bottle. I'm not sure what it was until this day, but it worked.

I believe that if people know that better choices and alternatives are available, they would choose to live and be happy. I only wanted to commit suicide because I saw no other alternative to the situation I was in. When people are brought to the knowledge that they do have healthy options and alternatives, they won't be self-destructive when things do go awry in their lives.

TO ALL MY SISTERS IN THE STRUGGLE

Chapter 3

SEXUALLY DYSFUNCTIONAL

I went through life, day after day, still hurt and depressed as ever, still waiting on God to send me someone or something to make this life worthwhile. But it never came. I experienced countless disappointments with each new relationship. "Oh, this one will work," I'd say to myself. And if that failed I'd say, "Well, I still have hope, this next one is sure to work out." However, this only brought continued disappointment. And each disappointment brought resentment toward the people involved, including myself. How could I be so dumb? How could I let this happen to me? I was taught better than this, I want better than this. What was I doing wrong? I now realize that I must have been listening to the wrong voice. I remember watching talk show after talk show about finding love. Each theme seemed to be, "If at first you don't succeed try, try, and try again - If you fall off that horse, just get right back on it!" But what they won't tell you is; if that horse has not yet been broken in, it will buck you off! And sisters, YOU cannot break that horse in, only GOD can!

By the time I was sixteen, a new trend in my life had begun. I was developing as a woman, and although my face was still unattractive to most, my body allowed many men to overlook that flaw. So, I was sexually harassed at school by the guys who I wanted to date or at least thought I wanted to date, and also by the old men in my neighborhood. I had mixed emotions of happiness and sadness based on this success and failure. Sisters, know that you are beautifully and wonderfully made no matter what any man, woman, or media outlet tells you. The media would have you believe that every girl who gets attention from guys is a size 4 with long straight hair. However, the guys give those girls attention because the media tells them too. God does not make junk, and he created you the way you are for a reason. Everyone does not like the same shapes and styles of people. Know that there is someone out there who will love you for who you are, not for who they or the media wants you to be. But trying to look at things on the bright side, I decided to make lemonade out of the lemons. Since they seemed to like me, I thought, "I might as well date them, it was better than nothing. Maybe God wants me to just take what He puts in front of me." Movies and the media fed a lot into this mistaken mentality. I would think of the romantic love stories about Prince Charming coming to save the day. I wanted all of that. I remember thinking, "My mommy told me I deserve it, so I'm going out there, and I'm going to make it happen with whomever God sends my way." This was my mindset. I was a person living in the real world trying to develop a fairytale and Hollywood lifestyle.

Not only did sexual dysfunction and abuse run rampant in my life, I also dealt continually with rejection. Again, it was mainly because I was told that my looks were not the greatest, but I had a "banging" body. Well, use what you got right? I was even taught that I could use this asset to attract men to church. I misunderstood the teaching. Although my ministry and church did not intend for me to date or sleep with any man who said I looked nice, I thought that was the way to get them to want a relationship with God. Hindsight is always 20/20, but when you're young, rejected by your peers, and alone, that seems like the best thing to do. I could meet my needs, the man's needs, and Gods needs. It was a win-win situation! Right? Only for some reason, after it was all said and done... maybe even months or a year later, my needs, and I'm sure Gods needs, were still left unmet. A physical relationship does not, nor ever will, replace the desire for a genuine relationship.

Continuing on, I decided to date one of the older men in my neighborhood. He was twenty-six and I was sixteen. He was a nice looking man and he could sing like nobody's business! This definitely attracted me, since I am also a singer. He had a job, which meant he could buy me things. And he had access to a car, or so he told me. So all systems were a go! I could have the love and romance I saw on TV, in movies, from my older sisters, and had heard about from my mom. The only problem was his age. And when my parents found out about his age, the relationship ended. My parents expected and wanted me to date someone my own age, so that's exactly what I did. I dated a roughneck teen with nothing but sex on his mind. I wasn't prepared for this type of bond, but he liked me, and was nice to me, so, oh well! Of course after I gave him my virginity, we didn't work out. I was taught to only give myself to my husband.

Although I really had no clue what I was getting into when I started having sex, I at least knew that he was suppose to be with me forever. However, I failed to let him know this before the fact. Of course, that's not to say that it would have changed his mind about taking my virtue. He could have easily lied and said that he would be with me forever to get in my pants, just as everyone else after him did. So now, my life was consumed with trying to correct mistakes that I'd made in my past relationships, all to no avail. The heartbreak continued; my goal of living the Fairy-tale/Hollywood life was coming undone, and I was struggling to hold it together. I'd wanted us to workout so badly. Sisters, this is one of the characteristics of the *Spirit of Heaviness*. This is called **Broken-Heart**.

The depression continued to set in. I was constantly in my room crying; tear soaked pillows became an everyday thing. I was so used to it that I, in a sick and twisted way, began to like the feeling of crying and seeing my sad face in the mirror. It was as though I gained comfort from being miserable because of what I'd allowed others to do to me. Sisters, this is also a characteristic of the *Spirit of Heaviness*. This is called **Self-Pity**.

The years went by and I swore I would never have sex again. It had caused so much physical and mental pain. Yet, I was still looking at the fairy tales, music videos, and romantic movies. I was still praying to God that true love would come my way, and soon! I thought, "If I could only find true love, then I would feel so much better and all the pain would simply go away."

The Enemy must have been having a field day by now. With my depression being high and faint thoughts of suicide, all I could do was pray and cry. And so I prayed and I cried. Eventually, I was sought out in high school by a classmate who was also a close friend of mine. We dated consistently in our junior and senior years. It was blissful, or so I thought, until his birthday came and his hormones came with them. It was a special day and although, again, I didn't want to have sex, I felt he deserved me. He had been with me all this time, bought me things, drove me places, and we never argued, why not give in to his desires? So, I did. Again in hindsight, I now know that we never argued because he always let me be right. The next day, I acquired an infection that took a week to clear up. I was livid! How could he do this to me? I told him about it, and he was so confused, and probably scared too. Imagine a teenage girl, in school taking pills to clear up something she couldn't even pronounce, trying to look normal in school while her body is irritating her to the point of tears. Sisters, this is another characteristic of the *Spirit of Heaviness*. This one is called **Physical Illnesses and Pains**.

It was a week before Christmas break when my boyfriend had to go out of town for the holidays. By this time I had forgiven him. I was madly in love with him, since he was the only one who stayed with me long term, and didn't initially just want me for sex.

While my boyfriend was out of town, I talked to him online, not knowing that he had decided to break up with me. He just didn't know how to tell me. When we'd discussed the issue, his argument was that I reminded him of a sister. A sister? After we had sex, I reminded him of a sister! Is this man sick or what? I cried into my pillow again. Then realizing it was the second semester of school and I wouldn't have a date for the prom, I really let the waters flow down stream! My semi-perfect life was crumbling again. "God, what do I keep doing wrong?" I would ask. Why do I deserve this? What can I do to fix this? I begged my ex-boyfriend to take me back, something my family would definitely not agree with, but he wouldn't, his mind was made up. Sisters, this is also a characteristic of the *Spirit of Heaviness*. This is called **Torn Spirit**[2].

At school, I had to look as though I was not affected by our break-up. I acted as though we were still friends. Somehow, I managed to get back in communication with the ex-boyfriend who I'd given my virginity to. I convinced him to go to the prom with me. He did go with me but I had a horrible time. I spent so much time trying to convince myself and the guy that had just dumped me that I was over him; that I went completely overboard. Some experiences happened that I would change, if I could turn back time. I would have gone to the prom with just the girls, ending with a girl's night out afterwards. Looking back, that was a real life lesson that I never want to happen to anyone else.

When does the vicious cycle end? The next day, my ex-boyfriend, who came to the prom with me, cut ties with me – again! "My God," I'd ask, "When does the heart break stop?" I know now that these breakups were for my good because God wanted me to get off of this sinful

---

[2] Proverbs 18:14

track. You see the Enemy can only do what God allows, and some people who would definitely turn your life down the wrong street, have enough sense to understand the scripture from Psalm 105:14-16: He permitted no one to do them wrong; Yes, He rebuked kings for their sakes, Saying, "Do not touch my anointed ones, and do my prophets no harm." So they back off, mainly to spare themselves of the wrath of God for messing with His chosen one. As a result of their fear of God, you and I are saved from the Enemy's complete destruction. There hath no temptation taken hold of you but such as is common to man. But God is faithful; He will not suffer you to be tempted beyond that which ye are able to bear, but with the temptation will also make a way to escape, that ye may be able to bear it: 1 Corinthians 10:13. This statement means that endured problems will make your strength increase and cause you to become a successful warrior for God. He uses people and circumstances to sharpen the skills and gifts that he'd put in your spirit before you were ever born. You must be trained and tested, in order to bring you to mastery level in your art and craft. It's the first rule of any martial arts instructor or business manager. Where do you think they got the idea?

While on this journey with me, you've seen the depression come and go as I've dealt with cheating, lying, and baffling boyfriends. I was a wreck as I continued looking for Mr. Right; I was a fantasy, fairytale, shipwreck waiting to go to shore. This is not good at all. I would go to church, pray, and then feel better, but when the next interested guy spoke to me, I was back on the love boat again, approaching shipwreck.

I now realize that I was begging God to send me love instead of asking Him to **be** my love. There is a big difference here. And my negative results show you how big the difference is. But because I took the wrong approach, I kept acquiring difficulties that I found to be almost unbearable.

TO ALL MY SISTERS IN THE STRUGGLE

Chapter 4

OLDER DOES NOT NECESSARILY MEAN WISER

When I went off to college, Oral Roberts University in Tulsa, Oklahoma, I left all the pain behind. God began to heal my broken heart. I had new friends of like faith. But I still didn't have a man to love me. However, this began to bother me less than it had before. I guess it's because I was preoccupied with actively seeking the things of God. I was in church 4 days a week. I was getting divine revelation of God and his purpose for my life. I began to write joyful songs and poetry. It was wonderful! I thought that I had finally gotten wiser about love, men, my needs and God's needs.

Then a guy came to campus that showed interest in me. I was reluctant, but the more he pushed, the more I fell for him. Needless to say, I fell hard. Unsuspectingly, after I left school for the summer to fulfill God's mandate to witness in a different area of the country, my new love found a new love interest; a girl at my church! After my arrival back to school, the first thing I saw was him with her. They were smiling and blushing at each other and looking so happy. "He didn't do that with me!" I screamed inside. This felt so surreal! I continued to think, "No wonder he didn't answer my calls that summer. I ran up my mom's phone bill; and this was why!" The denial of a real love continued. In hindsight, it was all for my good. He ended up getting a girl pregnant, and she had to leave school. And this was a girl who I was proud of, on fire for God, a young prophetess in the making. That could have been me! You see, the Enemy "don't care nuthin" about your gifts, as long as He can get you to turn away from God; He has you and will annihilate you! But I was protected by the **Master**!

Even though the pain of the breakups eventually made me break down, God protected me from a lot of bad decisions and men. God, I thank you and I love you so much! God will provide safety and security.

TO ALL MY SISTERS IN THE STRUGGLE

Chapter 5

THE GOOD WORKING

My own personal story of the struggle for love, in the wrong places, continued after college. With the same goal of being loved, I hooked up with a lying, deceitful, whoremongering preacher. He definitely had a gift and calling of God on his life, but we all do, so big deal. That gift was what drew me to him. To be quite frank, his true character showed up from the start of our relationship, and I tried to rationalize that away; to just over-look it. Thank God for divine intervention! He hooked up with someone else, broke my heart; and as I look back in retrospect, I couldn't have been so happy for that now! I pray that the young lady he is with still has a sense of God's calling on her life, as opposed to the slavery he had in mind for her. Also, I pray that he has been renewed in his mind while building a Godly character. I cried so much and was so confused over that situation, that I stopped going to church. I'm sure that this persistent, bad news excited the Enemy. I had become a threat to Him while ministering with this preacher, and I'm sure He had to take me down by enticing me to fall for him. I learned a lot from working in the ministry with this man. Sisters, you must know that every challenge conquered catapults you to a new level in God. I acquired **new weapons** to deal with future relationships and ministry tactics to defeat the Enemy. Unfortunately, I also experienced and gave in to new temptations and failed; thus, I experienced **new struggles**. But now that I know better, I will hold myself accountable based on my knowledge of areas where my flesh is weak. That new challenge will help me to battle future problems of this nature. God has brought me to a **new level**.

Romans 8:28 says: "And we know that all things work together for good to them that love God, to them who are called according to his purpose."

Do you see how I became more empowered with Godly wisdom after my experience with that character? It all worked out for my good. Well, if you don't see it, I do.

You may even be thinking now, "Natalie, you don't understand, I lost my mother when I was 10 years old." Or, "My father was shot in cold blood right before my eyes, and he wasn't in any gang. He never did anyone any harm."

To you I will say this; God still would not allow you to be tested in that area of your life if He didn't equip you with the strength to be able to overcome it. Remember, He put your gifts in you from **before** the womb. You may say as I did, "Well, He got the wrong one because I can't handle it. This is too much for me to bear." When this is happening God wants you to receive an upgrade. He desires for you to put on the whole armor of God; allow Jesus and the Holy Spirit to take control of your mind, body, and soul so that they can get you through tough times. In order to do this, you will need to walk closer with Him. This should result in maximized strength to do warfare with the Enemy.

Let's expound more on what I learned about weapons, struggles, and levels in God. Now that you have survived, its time to go to the next level; just like in a video game, whenever you reach a new level you have more gifts available to access, and stronger weapons to use in battle. Whereas, on the previous level it was called "firepower," on this next level it is called "mega-firepower." Where on the previous level you could only run from the Enemy, now you can fly. You now have additional weapons. Keep in mind that this in only in a video game that your weapons increase. In real life with the real Enemy, if you have given your life to Christ, you had the weapons all along at your disposal. Fortunately, it took that challenge to bring it out of you. They increase for a reason. Yes, you do have a bigger and tougher fight on your hands, but you also have more weapons, gifts, and tools to fight the Enemy with. You couldn't fly on the previous level, but on this one, you have the ability to fly if you grab hold of the right gift. That is another thing you will learn, just because you have the gifts doesn't mean you know when to use them. You have to grab hold of the right gift and the right weapon to get the right results. You can still overcome it, you just won't know until you start accessing the correct weapons. **Just because you haven't done it before, does not mean you can't do it now**! The *Holy Spirit* is your mentor, your supervisor, manager, and sensei. His job is to teach you how to succeed while you are on earth to effectively complete your calling.

So yes, God did allow your mom to die when you were 10, that's a part of your destiny; the level you get to after conquering that hurt and pain will allow you to minister to others in similar situations of that magnitude. The same goes for the guy whose father was shot at point blank range, and any other horrible situation someone has encountered. God has not left you.

He wants to make you stronger. Bad things happen to good people because this world is contaminated by sin. God doesn't want to take away your free will, He can, but He won't. That would upset the rules He put into effect. He sent his only son, Jesus, to redeem us from sin. It's up to us now to use that salvation to affect and infect others still bound by sin mentality.

My sister, God loves you more than you ever know. He is grooming you to reign, and just like most pets, we don't like to be groomed, but God knows more than we do about what we have need of, what we can handle, and what we can overcome. If you are not sure of any of this, I suggest you begin to do as much reading and listening to seasoned warriors who have been where you are, and where you are trying to go. It will make much more sense then, I promise you.

TO ALL MY SISTERS IN THE STRUGGLE

Chapter 6

NEVER RATIONALIZE YOUR DISCERNMENT

Even though I felt that I was stronger and able to resist temptations of the Enemy with the "new weapons;" I faced yet another crisis. This crisis was the catalyst and inspiration for this book. I was extremely vulnerable and still heartbroken over the preacher. I had ignored the Holy Spirit telling me that this man was not a good fit for the plan God had for my life. I was still in the same cycle of wanting to find my prince charming, the love of my life. The Devil had set a trap for me, and it seemed that I'd fallen for it every time!

His next trap was to send out the *Seducing Spirit*[3]. This Spirit took control over this weak, willing vessel. He infiltrated this young man's mind and convinced him to do things like:

- Lie Hypocritically
- Having a Seared Conscience
- Attractions/Fascinations to False Prophets, Signs and Wonders
- Deceive
- Cause Confusion
- Wander From The Truth
- Be Fascinated to Evil Ways, Objects, or Persons
- Seduce and Entice
- Control

The *Seducing Spirit* encouraged this new man in my life the act out on these thoughts. His charm was hypnotizing, so I let everything, my morals and values, along with my keen sense of judgment, just slide away. Sisters, don't ever do this!

There is a scripture I never really understood until my heart was broken into so many fragile pieces. Proverbs 4:23-27 says: "Keep vigilant watch over your heart; that's where life starts. Don't talk out of both sides of your mouth; avoid careless banter, white lies, and gossip. Keep your eyes straight ahead; ignore all sideshow distractions. Watch your step, and the road will stretch out smooth before you. Look neither right nor left; leave evil in the dust." I've learned that you should never tell

---

[3] 1 Timothy 4:1

anyone everything you're thinking, wanting, or feeling; no matter who it is. One must remember that all men are human, and they can use that information for their benefit, as opposed to yours. If you feel uneasy about sharing something personal with someone new in your life, you probably shouldn't. Listen to the *Holy Spirit of Truth*. He will often whisper things in your ear like: "Don't say that. Don't tell him or her that about you. He will even tell you things like, that man or lady is lying, he is not telling you the truth about where he has been. Or don't go over his house because this or that will happen." How many times have you heard something tell you to do or not to do something, but you ignored it? How many times have you rationalized it away? Now understand, sometimes the enemy speaks in your ear and causes you to panic or have anxiety about different events or people. I am not talking about those small instances when He is trying to unnerve you with lies and steal your peace. I am referring to the times when we know we are in an unhealthy situation, yet, we ignore the *Holy Spirit of Truth*[4] when He provides us with a way of escape.

Hawks look for their prey from way up in the air. They look for the weak and feeble, and the easy kill. Don't be the easy kill. I want to condition you, by the power of God and through my experience, to be strong enough to not be attacked and learn how to fight back.

---

[4] John 16:13

TO ALL MY SISTERS IN THE STRUGGLE

Chapter 7

HOW TO FIGHT BACK

Know Your Enemy!

Be watchful! For the Thief comes when you least expect it. He will try to wait until you are off your guard to attack. Always be ready to fight and don't give up any ground to Him; the Enemy doesn't deserve even an acre of your land!

"From the days of John the Baptist until now, the Kingdom of Heaven suffereth violence, and the violent take it by force." (Matthew 11:12) If you think in terms of boys fighting, it's a known, unspoken man-law to not hit below the belt. It seems as if we have taken this mentality into the spiritual world. Why is that? Wicked is wicked; wickedness hits below the belt, so then, you must hit Him where it hurts most, too. He's hitting you; punching you, going for the TKO, and enjoying every minute of it because of your lack of knowledge of true spiritual sportsmanship. Fight back, fight hard; fight for your life; there are no play fair rules in fighting for your life. The Kingdom of Heaven suffereth violence, so you violently take it back, BY FORCE, from the Enemy who is the self-proclaimed King of Darkness. Get your conquering spirit back, and defend your life; choose life over death!

Let me explain to you how to fight. God tells us in the Bible: The world is unprincipled. It's dog-eat-dog out there! The world doesn't fight fair. But we don't live or fight our battles that way—never have and never will. The tools of our trade aren't for marketing or manipulation, but they are for demolishing that entire massively corrupt culture. We use our powerful God-tools for smashing warped philosophies, tearing down barriers erected against the truth of God, fitting every loose thought and emotion and impulse into the structure of life shaped by Christ. Our tools are ready at hand for clearing the ground of every obstruction and building lives of obedience into maturity. (2 Corinthians 10:3-6)

How to fight the *Spirit of Rejection*

In the first chapter we learned about the pawns. We learned that they are used by the enemy to convince you that you do not belong or fit in. For this mission he sent out the *Spirit of Rejection*[5]. On his assignment he used rejection by others to convince me to reject myself, and then ultimately God.

Once I broke through, I realized that what everyone thought of me did not matter; whether it was boys, friends, family, and even myself. The only thing that mattered then and still matters now is what God, my

---
[5] Genesis 3:6-13

creator, thinks of me. He said that: For ye have not received the spirit of bondage again to fear; but ye have received the Spirit of adoption, whereby we cry, Abba, Father. (Romans 8:15) I will explain this more in the next chapter. For now, let us continue learning how to fight the other Spirits.

How to Fight the *Seducing Spirit*

Remember the *Seducing Spirit* that was used with my ex-boyfriend? Remember its characteristics? This one is fought off by knowing and speaking the truth that God's Holy Spirit gives you. When the Spirit of truth comes, he will guide you into all truth. He will not speak on his own but will tell you what he has heard. He will tell you about the future. (John 16:13) Listen to those whispers. Listen to those 'something told me'. He was sent here on purpose and is talking to you for a reason.

Round One

You should know that all men lie, whether they want to or not. They all lie. It's as though it is infused in their genetic makeup, since the fall of man. Why do they lie? That I can't answer. They don't even know. Let us ask Paul in the Bible. Consider his famous quote. "When I want to do good, evil is always present." Below is a passage taken from Romans 7:14-25:
> For we know that the law is spiritual, but I am carnal, sold under sin. For what I am doing, I do not understand. For what I will to do, that I do not

practice; but what I hate, that I do. If, then, I do what I will not to do, I agree with the law that it is good. But now, it is no longer I who do it, but sin that dwells in me. For I know that in me (that is, in my flesh) nothing good dwells; for to will is present with me, but how to perform what is good I do not find. For the good that I will to do, I do not do; but the evil I will not to do, that I practice. Now if I do what I will not to do, it is no longer I who do it, but sin that dwells in me. I find then a law, that evil is present with me, the one who wills to do good. For I delight in the law of God according to the inward man. But I see another law in my members, warring against the law of my mind, and bringing me into captivity to the law of sin which is in my members. O wretched man that I am! Who will deliver me from this body of death? I thank God—through Jesus Christ our Lord! So then, with the mind I myself serve the law of God, but with the flesh the law of sin.

Also, it is a common characteristic of men and women to lie to get what they want, regardless of whom they hurt. It's the lion's spirit in them, I guess. Lions want what they want, when they want it; regardless of who they hurt in the process. This lion can only be contained or transformed with the acceptance of Christ in their lives. Even then, they still do it. The difference is, however, that they now have a holy conscience to correct them. They may think twice before doing it, or at least apologize after doing it. I know it's sad, but it's true.

Just because it is a well-known fact that men lie, that in no way makes it okay. Lying from anyone is unacceptable and not okay for you to put up with. It's not alright for you to put up with the pain of being disrespected from anyone. And don't let your close relatives, not even your mother, advise you to do this. They may say words like this: "Just deal with it, "Girl, just get over it, don't you know that's the nature of the beast." Don't listen to this misinformation! I remember asking an ex-boyfriend this question, "Would you allow some man to lie to your daughter, to break her heart with deception? Would that be okay with you?" He didn't answer me which meant that I was right. My reply to his nonverbal was, "Treat me the way you would want a man to treat your daughter. He got the picture, for a few months time, anyway. Then he forgot again. Yeah, I can laugh about it now. It must also be said that I did not hold my ex-boyfriend accountable for his mistreatment of me, even after that talk. Everyone must be held responsible for their unhealthy actions toward you. I think men are so focused on the trials that they're involved in, that they don't take the proper time to consider how their actions affect their loved ones; however, that is still unacceptable.

My father was not very good at conveying his feelings to us in love. He would complain about what was not right, and how no one helped him. The pressures of the world were on his shoulders, but instead of coming home and leaving the pain outside on the front door mat, he, without realizing it, wiped the dirt on us. His family became the enemy. Now, my father loves us dearly and would never intentionally hurt us. But he didn't stop to consider his actions, and as a result, we were hurt and bruised badly.

Now, some men reading this book may say, "Oh, here we go again, another man-basher story. All of us are not like that." And he would be correct. So if the shoe fits... you know the rest of the saying – wear it! In my experience those who are complaining about man-bashing, in women songs and books, are actually the men doing the bashing. Those who are not may tend to think the songs and books are funny. We know that the Enemy doesn't like to be uncovered; no darkness enjoys to be brought out into the light. So, of course, He will use you to retaliate. Hey, it's the nature of the beast right? "Leave me alone!" those lions growl. Let's be truthful and expose the truth to reveal to good women that they deserve to remain in the queenly status that God has assigned them.

Second and Final Round

You don't **need** a human being's love the way that you think you do. God said in the King James Bible in Matthew 6:33– "But seek ye first the kingdom of God, and his righteousness; and all these things shall be added unto you." I think what He means is: fall in love with His will for your life, and then you will get what you want because He can trust you to not hurt yourself or others with what He gives you. It took me 21 years to realize that I had been looking for love in all the wrong places.

I tried to understand what the Seasoned-Saints and other family members meant when they would say, "Girl, you don't need a man," etc. but I just didn't get it. Unfortunately, I thought they just didn't want to see me happy, and as a result, I rebelled. All of my life I was looking for and trying to find ways to make people like me. It is a natural human instinct to need love and acceptance, the problem is that we seem to misinterpret the way we are to achieve this love and acceptance from others. What the Seasoned-Saints were trying to tell me was that, since I was single and had not yet found out my purpose in life, my number one priority should have been to "fine-tune" my relationship with God so that I could walk out my destiny. The traumatizing experience with my ex-boyfriend brought me to this hard hitting realization.

Good men know and want good strong, Godly women. My definition of strong is being able to do anything needed in your life without necessarily needing help from men. That not only pertains to work and financial stability, it also refers to emotional and mental stability; you must obtain these goals as you develop a personal relationship with Yahweh. Real men want women with morals, values, and etcetera. There's plenty of things they want, but that is not the focus of this book. As a matter of fact, that should not be your focus either. Let me try to break it down to you in plain Jane English. If you are single, the only person you should be in love with and trying to understand is GOD. If you are married, your spouse comes second to God. Now understand this, your spouse does not come second to your church or your ministry, he only comes second to your **personal relationship** with God. Now I know that sounds either:

A. So much like a cliché, if you grew up in church

Or

B. Just confusing or stupid to you, but don't give up on me and this book right now. Keep reading!

You may begin to feel "alone" or lonely as you are healing from your broken relationship. When I first decided to heal I began to feel *"Heavy"*. I need you to know that, that feeling will pass. Your body is going through withdrawal because what it once used to feel the void is no longer there. Let me reassure you that you **will** be ok. You must stay around healthy people during this time. Look at the topic below.

How to Fight off the *Spirit of Heaviness*

The *Spirit of Heaviness* is fought off by resting in the joy of the Lord. God says in Nehemiah 8:10 …Do not sorrow, for the joy of the LORD is your strength. Just shout and scream with joy for this reason. The Holy Spirit is also your comforter, which means you can talk to Him about whatever is going wrong in your life. Isaiah 61:3 says: To console those who mourn in Zion, To give them beauty for ashes, The oil of joy for mourning, The garment of praise for the spirit of heaviness; That they may be called trees of righteousness, The planting of the LORD, that He may be glorified. I know you're thinking that you can't see Him so how can you talk to Him. I used to think the same thing. Just because you can't see Him, that doesn't mean that He is not there. So smile my sister. Sometimes we have to sing, dance, or shout in spite of what's going on. If you're thinking you will look odd or feel odd, so what! It's about you feeling better about yourself and life by doing something that keeps you healthy and makes you happy.

TO ALL MY SISTERS IN THE STRUGGLE

Chapter 8

HAPPY/HEALTHY

The most important person on this earth is YOU. You may already know that but you don't understand it. If you did you wouldn't be in the situation you're in. So look, your purpose in life right now is to keep yourself in a status that I like to call: Happy/Healthy. I say this because important people in our lives may make us happy for the moment or several years, but are they healthy for us? Are situations that you put up with in your family, friends, children, co-workers, etcetera, healthy for you?

Some people are just "toxic" and you should not be around them while you are healing. I believe that if you are around people that always cause you to have bitter moments of, "I don't like how they did or handled this or that," then they are not healthy for you. They are "toxic" because they will frustrate you so much until your emotional level about the situation goes from good to horrible in 0.5 seconds! And don't lie to yourself or pretend that it doesn't happen. You know when you get that boiling feeling in the pit of your stomach, or that teary eyed feeling and knot in your throat. These are just two examples, but you have many other ways that your body tells you that you are in emotional danger and need to flee the situation for health reasons. Embrace these emotions because God would not have put them in you, if you didn't need them. Find out what the pain is telling you, and then execute a plan to stop it. Ignoring the problem won't make it go away. You've been trying to avoid it all this time and it hasn't helped, has it? So snap out of it and deal with the situation! Let's keep it real. And let's keep you real Happy/Healthy.

Let's go into more detail about the points I made in the previous section. Society has taught us to ignore our feelings, and in some cases, they tell us to embrace the wrong ones. For example: "If you can't be with the one you love, then love the one you're with; There is nothing wrong with a one night stand; I don't like him and he doesn't like me, but we can have sex."

Or

"I like him and if sex is the only way I can get him to stay around me, then it's better than nothing; Don't tell him or her that they made you upset when they said or did something to upset you; If you do, they won't talk to you anymore and you **need** their love; If I do everything I can for this person to make them happy, then that will make me happy."

This worldly characterization of how to behave in society is portrayed not just in soap operas but in commercials, songs, and all forms of media; it's like the world is screaming, "Get hurt and commit suicide. We want you to end up miserable from all the mistakes you will make!" And we freely give into their requests saying, "Ok, I'll do it, I will die for you."

What I want you to think about is this. Who is this YOU? And why are THEY allowed to tell you what to do with your life? More than that, who died and made THEM king?

The answer to these questions if you haven't come up with them on your own yet is this:

The 'YOU' is society.

> [6]Society defined is: group sharing interests: an organized group of people who share an interest, aim, or profession.

Why are THEY allowed to tell you what to do? They do it because we, or more specifically you, allow them to. Why are they in charge? No one died and made them king over your life but you. That's another problem we as hurting people from loves-lost have. We tend to make the ones we love King over our lives. Therefore, we make them "gods" in our lives. Why is that? I mean, if you want to be a rebel, as most claim to be in this century, rebel against this behavior. I like the song that Lauryn Hill wrote when she came to the realization of God as the source of her life. It's simply titled "Rebel." It's from her last publicly released album entitled, MTV Unplugged No. 2.0: Lauryn Hill.

---

[6] (Encarta, 1998-2004)

It's odd that while we are killing ourselves emotionally, mentally, and spiritually, we are also overdosing to rid ourselves of the symptoms. The medications out today, which people take for pain, are unimaginable. And if people are not on pharmaceuticals, they are self medicating with street drugs, alcohol, and sex.

I received some very pertinent information, during the aftermath of my crisis from a behavioral hospital, which I'd like to share with you.

Here are some keys to knowing what each emotion or symptom means:

Scared	**Hurt/Sad**	**Anger**	**Guilty**
Fear	Blue	Disgusted	Shameful
Anxiety	Despair	Indignation	Embarrassed
Nervous	Gloomy	Jealous	Humiliated
Panic	Discouraged	Bitter	Remorseful
Worried	Disappointed	Annoyed	Inadequate
Terrified	Lonely	Outraged	Disgrace
Distressed	Bored	Grouchy	
Timid	Helpless	Contempt	
Shy	Hopeless	Rage	
	Rejected	Hate	
		Irritable	
		Frustrated	

Unhealthy Emotions 1

[7]Scared- I am in danger
Hurt/Sad- I am helpless to met a need

---

[7] (H. Paul Stanley Jr., 2001)

Anger- I am being mistreated
Guilty- I am inadequate

These feelings were put in you by God and they should not be ignored. First, listen to them and take a positive and healthy approach to change the cause of the symptoms. Second, seek help as soon as you can. Last, change them into good feelings.

Here are some examples of what to look for in Healthy/Happy emotions:

Safe	**Happy**	**Affectionate**	**Grace**
Optimistic	Joy	Sympathetic	Accepted
Trusting	Cheerful	Forgiving	Loved
Secure	Content	Tolerant	Forgiven
Calm	Enthusiastic	Love	Adequate
Confident	Amazed	Caring	Important
Brave	Hopeful	Warmth	Clean
Powerful	Encouraged		Sufficient
	Pleased		Belonging
	Elation		
	Serene		

Healthy Emotions 1

Safe- I am taken care of
Happy- My needs are being met
Affectionate- I am being treated well
Grace- I am adequate

Did you notice that when you change those negative feelings, the feelings that should replace them are the exact opposite?

Okay, so now you may still be feeling or thinking, "Wow all this sounds good, really good, and I want to let him go and just love God with all my heart, but I don't see how. I mean I know it's the right thing to do but my heart won't let me." I felt the same way, for twenty-one years of my life, and I am twenty-seven as I write this book. But let me tell you, it is possible. This is what worked for me. I am not saying it will definitely work for you because everyone is different, however, you might as well start here. Remember, you've tried everything else your way, and look where it's gotten you.

TO ALL MY SISTERS IN THE STRUGGLE

Chapter 9

THIS IS MY STORY

It seems like it all began when I was 5 or 6 years old. I was in kindergarten or first grade and had a traumatizing experience in the restroom. At this particular school, our restroom was connected to our classroom. The teacher was absent that day and we had a substitute. It was towards the end of the day and by that time the substitute teacher decided that it was time for her nap. I got up from my table and woke her up to ask for permission to go to the restroom. She said, okay but then she went right back to sleep. While I was in the restroom, a little boy in my class came in, turned out the light, and kissed me. I fought him off by pulling his ear (it was the only thing I could find in the dark). That was enough to get him out of the room with me. I cleaned myself up and came out the bathroom. When I told the substitute what happened, she woke up again and just said, "Ya'll stop playing." That event would shape what the Enemy thought would be His destiny for me. I went home and told my parents but since I had fought back and had told the teacher, my job was done. What else could I or anyone else have done? Since I fought back and alerted the adult figure in charge, they figured the problem was solved. I seemed to be okay and not shaken up too much about it. However, I wasn't okay, and I didn't know that I'd been hurt so deeply by it.

Through recent therapy, I was helped in realizing that those types of events and others that I'd experienced were not okay. I learned that negative actions require consequences, especially those that inflict pain or discomfort on others. Additionally, since strong action was not taken against these men, requiring them to face punishment for what they had done to me, it wasn't okay. It doesn't matter whether they were young, old, church goers, or a different nationality. My parents and I were too nice! Sometimes you have to put "nice" aside and let justice be served. It doesn't mean that you love God and his people any less. It means that you love God's property (yourself) more. You should ALWAYS come first. Always? Yes, ALWAYS!

Yes, I let things slide because I wanted to appear as the nice one; the one who may not have been as pretty as her siblings, but got along with everyone including their rivals. I wanted this characteristic to make me special and beautiful. But guess what, you don't always know what's best for you.

My traumatic event caused me to take a deep, long look at my life. So, I know you are wondering, Natalie what happened to you? What was so traumatizing that it inspired you to get sick and tired of being sick and tired? What gave you the strength and courage to write this book? What was my traumatic event? I knew you wanted to know. You are so nosey! But all fun aside, here is my life's testimony. I've given you a look into the pawns of my suicidal and sexually dysfunctional childhood. This is the episode that landed me in jail for a night and in the hospital for a month.

Well, the last false intimate relationship with a supposed man of the cloth caused me to re-evaluate my belief and faith in God. Why did this keep happening to me? Why did I always end up wanting more out of the relationship than the man? I even questioned God directly, "Why God, did you give me this desire and these feelings if no one will reciprocate them to me?" Then I began crying for what I thought would be my last time. I got up, cleaned my face, and drove to the store around midnight; not really wanting to shop for food, just walking, trying not to think anymore. Suddenly, I was approached by a charming black man who told me everything I ever wanted to hear. It was like he had been in the bedroom hearing my cries to God. I was skeptical but willing to give it a try. I even thought, "From now on, I am only dealing with men that have the same mindset and goals as I have."

I began to quiz Mr. Charming, in the store, hoping that would cause him to leave. "Where do you work? What college did you graduate from?" Many of his answers met my qualifications and the ones that didn't, well, he'd smooth talk them out with an answer like, "I'm currently working on that now."

I had goose bumps all over. Had I finally met my mate? On the heels of a catastrophic and twisted relationship with a man of the cloth, had my prince come? Had my ship finally come in? Surely, this was God smiling down on me. I was so excited. I got into my car, after this "prince charming" packed my things away into the trunk, and I sped home to call my oldest sister. The tone of her voice was anything but pleasant. I didn't understand why. She knew the hurt I had just experienced, and yet she was not happy for me. "She never wants to see me happy," I thought.

I didn't have a heart to heart conversation with her until three years later. If only we both had known how to explain our side of the situation, maybe, I wouldn't have gotten so involved. But who knows, what's done is done and I am better for it. I ended up dating this "prince charming" for roughly three years. He had not been accepted by my family; therefore, I became stressed. Because of the stress, I experienced dramatic hair loss; this was a huge concern because my hair was short and fine to begin with. In addition to that, I gained ten pounds from consuming fatty foods that he fed me that I normally wouldn't have eaten. I also became pregnant. Unfortunately, I had an ectopic pregnancy, thereby, suffering a miscarriage. During this time, I was proud of myself for having purchased my first home. I'd allowed him to "stay over every night" as opposed to moving in with me. He would come home late and sometimes not at all. That was his way of lying to me and to himself about being dedicated to our relationship. I'd stopped praying and fasting. I mean why bother? I would only pray for a better life and it seemed like I had finally gotten what I prayed for. The most I continued to do was thank God for the life I had, which was not the praying I needed to be doing. Before the first year was up, I'd already met his mother, who considered me her daughter, and he'd affectionately call me his wife. I was a little afraid of this good treatment; it had never happened before. No one had charmed me the way he did.

Something was missing from this relationship that I couldn't quite put my finger on. But it continued to bother me. Remember those signs I taught you about earlier in the book, these are the signs I began to ignore:

1. The fact that he had just gotten out of jail on a robbery charge.
   Symptoms I felt: Numb
   Message from Symptom: My senses were dulled

2. The fact that he had just had a baby (just days after we started dating) by his ex-girlfriend, who he used to live with.
   Symptoms I felt: Nervous and Irritable
   Message from Symptom: Scared and Anger
   Meaning: Scared- I am in danger
   　　　　　Anger- I am being mistreated

3. The fact that he currently did not have a car and was living with a friend.
   Symptoms I felt: Annoyed and Worried
   Message from Symptom: Anger
   Meaning: Anger- I am being mistreated

4. The fact that he would not come home and would get upset when I called him to ask why.
   Symptoms I felt: Fear, Anxiety, Nervous, Panic, Worried, Terrified, Distressed, Lonely, Blue, Rejected, Despair, Disappointed, Rage, and Frustrated
   Message from Symptom: Scared, Hurt/Sad, Anger
   Meaning: Scared- I am in danger
         Hurt/Sad- I am helpless to met a need
         Anger- I am being mistreated

5. The fact that he always had another "roommate" to stay with so he wouldn't have to live with me.
   Symptoms I felt: Jealous, Frustrated, Lonely, Rejected, Blue, and Anxiety
   Message from Symptom: Scared, Hurt/Sad, Anger
   Meaning: Scared- I am in danger
         Hurt/Sad- I am helpless to met a need
         Anger- I am being mistreated

6. The fact that he did more talking than showing me that he would marry me…some day, or as soon as he got everything together, as soon as he made more money, etc.
   Symptoms I felt: Worried, Hopeless, Discouraged, Annoyed, Frustrated
   Message from Symptom: Scared, Hurt/Sad, Angry
   Meaning: Scared- I am in danger
         Hurt/Sad- I am helpless to met a need
         Anger- I am being mistreated

7. The fact that I never saw him go to school.
   Symptoms I felt: None
   Message from Symptom: I was too in love to notice.

Yes, I could go on and on with all the signs that I saw, yet, ignored. I could get past all that, right? "Everyone has a past, and the other things that bothered me were material, and I'm not superficial," I thought. And yes, I ignored all the signs, all the warnings, all the family silence to be with the one I loved. When you ignore those feelings that your body is giving you, it only gets worse. Your body is screaming "Fire! Fire! You were not built to handle this situation, or we certainly can't handle it right now, so flee!" But I was thinking, "Flee? Where would I go? Who will I go to? He is the first and only person, in my adult life, who has shown me true love. Surely it's not worth giving up over some weird feelings." I continued to hold on to his promises, to hope for his success and dreams for my sake. I even went as far as calling my friends for advice. Between my ex-boyfriend's persuasive wiles, my family's silence, and advice from friends, I didn't know that to do. I became so confused that I couldn't separate fact from fiction. I wanted to believe him. Just because someone **tells** you something is true, does not mean it is accurate. When someone SHOWS you who they are, believe them, at that moment. Don't believe anything they say or do that's contrary to what they have already shown you, everything else is just a smokescreen. Remember, out of the abundance of the heart the mouth speaks, especially in times of frustration.

Now don't get me wrong, I am not bashing men nor am I bashing my ex-boyfriend. I just want you to learn and know how to judge the true character of people. He really wanted to be good to me. He, in no way, meant to cause me any harm; he even told me this on several occasions. The problem between us was his overpowering character. What he intended to do was overcome by his character, and his character, just like your character, directs your life. Like many young men who were raised without a true father figure or Godly influence, he didn't know how to be a Godly man. So why was I telling him to be one? You can't turn a frog into a prince; this is not the fairytale of "The Frog Prince!" The world's way to get a happy ending is certainly not God's way. A man is only going to change for God when He realizes that he can't do it without God. Sisters, you are not his God or his mother. Let that man grow up and become a man **on his own**, preferably without you around; that way, you know it is a true change in his character and not just his charming face and behavior when he is around you.

I remember the first time I saw my ex-boyfriend without me around his family. I was so hurt and disappointed to see them drinking and smoking after a funeral, like that was the life. What I had to understand was that was his life. I had to understand that he and his family had a different lifestyle than the one which I was accustomed to. I'd finally seen his true, ungodly character. He told me later on that he had two ways of living; he likes how he lives with me, and he likes the way things are with his family, that's why he only visits them when necessary. He kept me confused. Did I fall for it? Of course I did! I wanted us to work. I would later find out that I just wanted love to work.

Remember, I told you that all men lie, they even lie to themselves. They can't help it. That sin nature is something else, and it takes the faith of God to replace that in the heart, or maybe replace the entire heart!

Let's move on to two recent events. During the entire time of our relationship, I never wanted to admit he had been lying to me. He was so charismatic that he could slide his way in and out of a lie in less than sixty seconds. Amazing for a young man, isn't it? Whomever he had learned these tricks from had taught him well; I was putty in his hands. Was I dumb to believe him? Umm, not necessarily. You see, I have a gift that my mother calls the gift of mercy. It causes me to look beyond who people are at the moment; and look at their potential. Since that mercy gift was coupled with an emotionally confused, desperate, and naïve young lady who was seeking love from the wrong source, man, the Enemy used it to His advantage. I told you He doesn't care anything about your gifts. But don't worry; eventually, I started to wise up.

Two years later, I was very upset that he'd driven my car to work without telling me. I had a friend take me to his job to get my car. When he got home, I was livid! He didn't say anything. He just went into the back room, then he came back up to the living room and pushed me over the couch. I was already upset so, instinctively, I pushed him back. He got the message not to lay a hand on me again, or so I thought. Remember what happened with the boy and me in the bathroom at school? It was the same scenario with a different cast. Just because I fought back did not mean that other repercussions and consequences should not have happened, they should have! But since I was taught to fight back, I again, thought my job was done. I left and drove to work. When I got home early that morning, he was packing his belongings and said he was leaving me. I tried to pray and cry, but no tears would come out. Now, I have to admit here, I am no angel. Part of me tried to put a guilt trip on him by crying to make him stay. Needless to say, it didn't work. He stayed the night with me, and I thought I had won, but that was just for him again. You see, I didn't realize that every time I allowed a man take sexual advantage of me, I wasn't getting LOVE; he was getting LAID. He left, of course, after he'd gotten his fix, and I was the one who had lost at love, again.

We had a very unstable relationship, even after he had moved out and gotten his own place. I can recall an evening when I stopped by his house just to say hi. He was so angry that I came to his house uninvited, that he snatched me up by my hair while yelling at me to leave. I did nothing because he kept calling me weak, and I wanted to prove to him that I could endure this type of pain from my man. Even now, I can't imagine how I'd allowed him to abuse me like that. Maybe, once again, I was too nice while focusing on trying not to lose him. Obviously, my niceness had not been working from the onset of our relationship. I couldn't even get him to attend church with me. I must admit that my encounters with men had been disastrous up to this point, so I thought I could keep him by letting him hit me; you know, try something new. It was completely wrong thinking. And sisters, when you can't get your man to attend church; look at the red flags, and run! The only one who can change people is God.

Sometimes, actually most times, God keeps people away from you for a reason. Those past relationships ended as they should have. Those guys saw the Spirit of God in me, and it brought out the darkness in them. Since dark and light can't bond together, they knew that I was not the one for them. I am so grateful to God for shielding me from a lot of those demons that were on assignment. The prayers of the righteous availed much! I know that this sounds strange but, I had to go through these trials in order for me to listen to God about His direction for my life.

Now, what landed me to the point of writing this book was a nervous breakdown. I finally found out the hard way that the love of my life was cheating on me. I had tried so hard to forget about him in times past. We would break up, and he would always come back to me. I saw this as his realizing what he truly wanted, that was very naïve of me; I was what he wanted, at that moment. I assumed that our relationship was exclusive, because he assured me that marriage was definitely in our future. Then, one day he asked me to experiment with other men and women, and to date as much as possible to make sure he was who I wanted. Naturally, I was perplexed by this suggestion. I didn't want to experiment, especially with marriage in my future! A few months later, I caught up with an old flame and he took me out to dinner. Now, thinking about what my ex-boyfriend had said a few months earlier, I decided to get in another relationship. We began to date. That ended abruptly when I was **raped** by him in my home. Since I was dazed and didn't realize what had happened, and my ex-boyfriend and I were still close, I decided to confide in him what had just happened. I showered, and then drove to his house, hoping he was available to talk. We talked all night and he came home with me. He told me that he wanted to make sure I didn't get hurt again. I was so shocked because I didn't expect him to want to start seeing me exclusively again. The next day he helped me set up for a party I had at my house. After that, he jumped in his friend's car and left. I thought everything was golden after that night. We were back together! Or so I thought. During the few months that my ex-boyfriend and I had stopped talking, I had learned how to be independent while enjoying hanging out with friends. Even though I didn't realize I'd been raped, I didn't want to risk it for a second time. My ex-boyfriend was the only person I would let touch me. Our new found romance was lovely; from text messages saying, "I love you," to out of town phone calls saying how much he missed me. I felt like I was in Heaven; the awful parts of our relationship were healing, even though he wasn't always around. Then the truth came out; absence makes the heart grow fonder, right? Negative! When he wasn't around, he was cheating on me. Sisters, just because a man is not around you, that don't necessarily mean that he is cheating, but it also doesn't necessarily mean that's not the case. The relationship was the opposite of heavenly as it began to spiral downward. A few months later, I allowed him to spend the night with me, even though it was against my wishes. That night, I started receiving continuous phone calls where no one would speak; so I just ignored them. The next morning, as I left for work, he asked me to take him to the store instead of home. He still didn't have a car after 2 1/2 years of our dating. The calls from the previous night resumed after I dropped him off. That's when I started to face facts. I lost my concentration at work, and when I got off, I went straight to his house to get some answers. I was worried and confused. Something was telling me that today would be the day I got my answers; but I didn't want to believe what I was feeling. I didn't want to believe that this was the end of our relationship. Now, I'm not telling you the entire story, only the parts that I feel will help you if you were to be in a similar situation.

When I arrived at his house and knocked on the door, a girl answered it. "She must be a relative," I thought. I asked for him, still positive about my initial thoughts. He requested that we go in a back room to talk, away from that girl. When I talked to him, I was nervous, shaking, trembling. He started to make small talk, but I finally convinced him to tell me the truth. I couldn't handle the truth! I became so angry and things got really chaotic. I attempted to pour his drink on him and to leave, but he grabbed me. So many things happened so quickly after that. It seems so *foggy*, hard to explain, and I don't really want to relive that experience. But I'll tell you that *I remember being knocked unconscious, I remember fighting back, I remember being called everything but a child of God by someone who I thought, was the love of my life, I remember the pain from his knee in my neck, the confusion from the names I was being called, and him blowing loveless kisses at me as he held me down, I remember red blood, I remember the police that I'd called, I remember the handcuffs, I remember the people I'd met in prison, the prostitutes who had similar stories but decided to make rape a way of living, I remember the other girls, all so much younger than me, who had fought back against physical abuse, yet ended up sitting in front of me as we waited to get our pictures taken. I remember the phone calls to family, lawyers, and anyone who would listen to me for help. I remember the young lady in the bottom bunk bed of my cell at the end of the hall who lullabied me to sleep with her praise and worship songs. Yes, I remember that jail is not a place I want to ever go back to. But I know it was all for my making, and because of that, I came out of the fire as pure gold.*

After my night in jail, I managed to get enough money to bail myself out. I went straight to the hospital, checked in, and stayed there about a month. I am referring to a mental health hospital. It was the best thing that ever happened to me. I learned so many things there. It was worth every insurance dollar. They taught me things about life and destiny that make more sense when applied to the word of God. I learned to value my life, know my purpose, and to seek my destiny.

With the help of trained therapists, I was able to realize my priorities. Becoming Happy/Healthy became the most important thing to me. I never want to end up in that situation again. Although I met some really interesting women in jail and learned a lot in the hospital, I'd rather be living my destiny. So with that said, here is what I learned that truly propelled me to give up on lost hopes, loves, and dreams that were unhealthy for me.

First

I met a beautiful young lady who had three gorgeous kids, and although she was mentally ill like me, she possessed great wisdom. She was my best friend in that hospital, and I pray for her often. She said to me, "Remember how you fought like hell to go see him? How you put off doing things that were important to spend time with him, and how you called him so much and thought about him every second? Well, try that hard to do the opposite, and don't let anything or nobody stop you." Since I am a Christian and a true believer in God (Yahweh), I took that to mean this: I have decided to put all the positive energy that I wasted on Mr. Wrong into loving and serving God since He is the only one who has:

- never abused me
- never talked down to me
- never hurt me
- never cheated on me
- never lied to me
- never stole from me
- never raped me

I believe that He is trustworthy and deserving of my love.

I began to realize and appreciate the wisdom of the Seasoned Saints and my family. Before now, their knowledge had not made sense to me. They would say, "God is the only one you should put your trust and love in. He will never leave you nor forsake you." It all began to make sense. I began to cry with tears of joy as I came to this eternal revelation. "God, this is what you've been trying to tell me? All these years I was looking for love in all the wrong places. I was just hurting myself, and it was all because I was trying to find you in the wrong places!"

Sisters, you have no idea how happy I am now. After all I've been through, no man on this earth will ever compare to how much God loves me. I've endured so much heartache, heartbreak, and so much rejection. That was the story line of my life up to the point of my breakthrough. You see, when we are young, we seldom realize the seeds the Enemy is sowing into our lives. For me, it took a nervous breakdown, hospitalization in a mental ward, prayer, and trained therapists to dig up those seeds of destruction to help my healing to begin. The therapists would say, "Look at what was sown here, this is no good. Let's throw this one away, okay?" Then they would replace the bad seed with a good one. If you're a true believer in God (Yahweh), this seed is cultivated by your constant trust in Him, prayer, and the reading of His word. Then you realize as you read, "Hey, that's the same thing my therapist told me." Biblical scripture tells us that: "And ye shall know the truth, and the truth shall make you free." (John 8:32) Wow! Isn't God wonderful? I truly love that Spiritual Man! Anyway, let me get off of my soapbox about my wonderful Husband who is my new first love. Now, let's get back to the story. That was the first thing that helped me to stay focused on changing my lifestyle, renewing my mind, repenting, and turning back towards God.

Second

The second thing that helped me was a session that a therapist had with our class at the hospital. This was truly a healing experience. She asked us to visualize this scenario, and as you read this section, I want you to do it to. Have someone read this part to you slowly as you do each step.

[8]Imagine that you are in a field.
In this field there are airplanes.
One of them is yours.
You see people you know get into other airplanes that are in a circle.
You get in your airplane, close the door, and begin to take off.
As you look down, you see your other friends taking off too.
You begin to fly opposite of the direction they are going over the green grassy field.
As you fly, you come upon a neighborhood.
A house looks familiar to you.
It is the house you grew up in when you were eight years old.
You decide to land and take a look inside.
As you open the door, you notice a family sitting at the table eating dinner.
It is your family.
You look for your eight year-old self at the table.
You see the expressions on their faces.
You remember how you felt at that table.

---

[8] (Wakeshider-Cruse, WestCott, & Bradshaw)

You realize that you have to tell yourself something very important, something they will need to know for the future.

When everyone else goes to bed, you go in her bedroom and quietly lean down beside the bed.

You tell her something quietly, so as not to wake the others in the house with the message.

You assure her that everything is going to be ok; you only want to protect her.

You fold back the covers, and pick yourself up.

You hug yourself tightly, and tell yourself that you are going to protect her.

You give her the message that you've wanted to tell her.

As you embrace, you realize that you must get back home.

You have to make a decision to either take the child with you, or leave her there.

You get back into your airplane with the child, or you put the child back into the bed, and cover her up again.

You get back into your airplane, and you take off.

You're flying back over the grassy fields now.

You see familiar places from your present time.

You land the plane back in the circle of planes, and you see your friends getting out, some with children, and some without.

The ones with children pick them up and pull them close as the children goes inside them and become them.

Now open your eyes. Think about what happened and how that child felt. Tell the person who read this part of the book to you. Make sure you journal this experience.

I hope this helps you like it helped me. This only encouraged my breakthrough. I ended up posting notes on all the mirrors in my house telling myself the message I told that child.

When the Enemy attacks me, or I simply have a negative thought to go back to the empty way that I used to feel, I remember the promise that I made to that little girl. I will never let her down; she doesn't deserve it, not from me and not from anyone else. I refuse to see her cry again in me!

That voyage was powerful for me. Prayerfully, it will be for you, as well. You may not be able to love the younger you. Maybe you do not like the way you acted at that age, and can't even see yourself trying to have a conversation with that child. If this is the case, try to think of another child in your life. Maybe it is someone who you love dearly and want to protect with all your might. This may be your own child, niece, nephew, or grandchild. This may be a hurting child that you see in the news or in other countries. How would you want to treat her/him? Would it be okay with you if someone took advantage of her or him? Would you feel upset, angry, sad, or hurt? If you saw this child about to hurt herself/himself, what would you do? What would you tell the child? If you can relate to this, treat yourself the way you'd treat that child, also, make sure others treat you this way.

Those are the two main things I used to begin my transition. I would implore you to consider a mental hospital if you have lost control and can't get your life together. It's funny how we don't have a problem going to the medical doctor, but as soon as we have a mental breakdown, it becomes taboo to get it fixed!

Let's be honest, sometimes when you don't feel well you need some medicine with your prayer, especially, if you're so far gone that your faith isn't where it needs to be. Get evaluated and tell them the truth. The psychiatrist gives the medicine and the therapist helps you heal, while the medicine numbs the pain and the symptoms. I recommend that if you have to take medicine, don't do it without therapy. If nothing else, at least just do the therapy. There are things that God allows the psychiatrist and therapist to see that you or your family can't see, even your friends for that matter. So, go get healed, okay?

TO ALL MY SISTERS IN THE STRUGGLE

Chapter 10

STAYING HEALED

After the healing begins, you have to devise a plan or strategy to keep progressing. No one wants to be or should be in and out of the hospital all the time. You have to set goals to keep yourself from sliding back into your past, and you have to measure yourself by them. I would recommend that you measure your goals once a month.

Just think about that word LIFE. In order to truly live a successful life, you have to stay healthy. Now are you beginning to understand why I say you have to keep yourself Happy/Healthy? I thought you would. See, I told you it would all make sense if you just stayed with me.

There are five areas of your life that I want you to consider: the Physical, Spiritual, Mental, Financial, and Social.

Physical

We have all heard about ways to maintain the physical; work out, stay in shape, and eat the right foods. Although we all know this, we seem to have trouble accomplishing it. In order to successfully accomplish maintaining the physical, you have to set obtainable goals in this area. And I mean truly obtainable! For example, one of my goals is to incorporate more fruit and vegetables in my diet. I'll try to eat at least one serving of fruit and vegetable a week. Once I have accomplished that goal, I will set new goals resulting in me eating the U.S. Department of Agriculture (USDA) suggested amount, seven days a week, out of habit. There is a food pyramid that was developed by the USDA which is an excellent tool to help you make healthy food choices. The food that you eat plays a big part in how you feel. Certain foods stimulate the mind. An additional realistic goal that I want to set for myself is to work out at least once a week. It even helps to take a brisk walk; this stimulates the mind, as well. Another important physical habit is rest. You should give your body ample time to recoup and process everything you have going on. Make sure you set aside at least one day a week to just relax, do nothing, don't go anywhere, and don't hang out with anyone.

Social

Here is where you can hang out with others, but I caution you to make sure that they are healthy to be around. Remember, some people won't want to hang out with you once you began to transition from your old destructive habits to your new productive ones; so you don't have to worry about avoiding them. However, when you begin to make new friends, watch and listen closely to what their conversation is about. If it is not beneficial to you and your destiny, or pleasantly relaxing, then gracefully bow out.

Spiritual

Since, I am a true believer of the existence God, I know that I have to talk and listen to Him daily. I make it a point to stay slowly in his presence. How do you stay slowly in His presence? You stay slowly in His presence by making it a point to not get so caught up in the hustle and bustle of the day; where you can't hear His voice. Also, I know that when I neglect to fellowship with God's family, my thoughts become more negative. This is why I make it a habit to attend church at least once a week; although I'd benefit more, if I attended twice a week. I also study God's word to learn more about Him and why I should continue to trust Him; this way, I have sharper weapons and tools to use when the Enemy attacks me with foolishness like, "You don't deserve God's love" or "You should find love another way." Reading God's word also teaches me other things, like how to train myself by listening to His Holy Spirit. His Spirit helps me to be obedient, to stay prayerful, and to fight off demonic attacks that I may encounter. Yes, I said demonic; if you don't believe in the spiritual world, you had better start doing so. It's amazing how other nations believe in the spiritual world and the Enemy; however, it seems like most Americans fail to or refuse to even acknowledge the existence. Doesn't that seem odd? That should tell you that you're missing out on something important. I talked about this in chapters 2, 6, and 7. Right now you may not be ready for it all, but believe me; you will need to get ready soon.

The Matrix; The Last Dragon; The Lion, The Witch and The Wardrobe; and Lord of the Rings are all movies that helped me get my mind focused on conquering. I'm sure there are more, but I think these are great movies to help you realize your destiny because they helped me to get mentally prepared. Although they are Hollywood fictional, Sci-fi movies, you can figure out fact from fiction and draw religious parallels.

Mental

Keep your mind sharp. If you didn't graduate high school; go get your GED! It will really boost your self-esteem. Getting your education not only helps you to stay on top of your game in this world, but it is also beneficial for self improvement. I must tell you the truth, I am smart, but I am also lazy; or at least I try to be. God and His Holy Spirit won't allow me to be that way anymore. It's interesting too, because I always hear them telling me, "No ma'am, do that over." This is definitely a good thing because He has motivated me to get a technical certification, teach school, apply for new jobs, and to learn more in my technical field. And I have to say that I feel like an overachiever. Moreover, I also know and expect to get paid my worth in the job market. The job market is tough for everyone, even those of us with degrees, but the difference in me now from before, is that I know how valuable I am in the workforce. I'm able to express it when I'm interviewed by a potential employer.

Now, keep in mind when you began to work out your goals, you will have "Haters." People that were your close friends and some of your family members may no longer want to talk to you. But to be honest, you probably won't even notice, because you will be too busy working out your destiny! Smile! This is definitely a good thing; not only that, but you will began to make connections with successful people who God will allow to help you achieve your goals. Now, a word of caution, do not get caught up in these people. They are human and can hurt you just like the last ones did. God is the only one who will never hurt you or sell you out for a promotion or any other gain. So, realize that they are only there to pass you batons on your track meet to your destiny. There will be some people whose jobs are to just be in the stands cheering you on. But remember, some fans don't stay for the entire game, they have other commitments, some are only assigned to watch you via the media, some will be pretentious and just hang around as a fan but in truth; they are cheering for the opposing team. So, don't take it personally, okay? Paul says, in from the Bible, Hebrews 12:1-3 "Keep running your race." Additionally, remember what he said in 1 Peter 4:12-13, "Do not think it strange that these things are coming against you…; they came against the Son of Man, too." Yeah, it comes with the territory, and since you are now living with the truth, you now have a huge territory to battle; but you are not alone.

Financial

Two things
 1. Stop Being Greedy.
 2. Stop Being Lazy.

I'm speaking from experience; some of us, maybe most of us whether believers or not, are greedy. There are two reasons for this, either we aren't used to having an abundance; so we keep it all to ourselves in fear that we will never get another thing, or we are evil-hearted with no intent to give to others. Either case is a horrible sin. God didn't create you to be selfish. He gave willingly to us, and so we must also give willingly to Him and others.

I'm reminded of the parable Jesus told of the men with the talents. The master gave them some money and one did not do anything with it. The master said, "Why are you acting so stupid? You are a bad steward and not ready to handle my wealth. Let me give it to someone who is." And that is what He did. (Matthew 25:14-29) This parable that Jesus told of, from the days of old, teaches about a rich man who is about to take a journey. He entrusted and allocated some of his wealth to three of his servants based on their abilities. The first was trusted with five talents, the second with two talents, and one talent was given to the third. The story goes on to tell how the first two servants quickly invested their employer's money. The third one did not invest his portion at all; instead he dug a hole in the ground and buried it. After the master had returned, the first two eagerly met him in delight to share the news of the great return on his money. They both were commended as "good and faithful servants." The master was well pleased, they were rewarded with increased responsibilities, and then they celebrated. However, the lazy third one was handled in a different way. He'd come to the master with the original talent that had been entrusted to him with no increase or return on his master's money. As a matter of fact, in these inflationary times, that money would likely be worth less than its value like the Dollar is to the Euro. He blamed his lack of motivation (laziness) on His master with a sad excuse like, "oh master I was so afraid to risk investing your money, you are such a harsh and cruel man, you're demanding and you expect to gain where you haven't toiled, so I hid the money to keep it safe until your return. And I'm so sorry that there is no increase to report." The master reprimanded him for being unproductive and lazy. He took his talent from him and gave it to the one who earned ten talents. The lazy servant was cast into outer darkness. What lesson should you learn? We must be good stewards of God's (our Creator's) money. If you see yourself here, say, "amen or say ouch," repent, and make the change; and it's not hard to make that change. Sisters, you can't just say, "I saw these half-priced shoes in the mall, and I had to have them!" or "I only spend my money on everyone else, so that's good, right?" No. Impulsive behavior is problematic. You must get control or it will control you. We see people on television and in the media everyday with these types of issues. They seek the help of professionals to get a grip on their problems. We know that one of the first steps to solving a problem is to admit that you have one. Now, if you have trouble stopping the negative behavior, then you need to seek help from others because there is obviously something wrong in your mind. And that's okay. It just needs to be fixed so that you will be able to make the right decisions to heal, and to live the life that God has intended for you, in victory.

No matter how you feel, you must get healed. Sisters, you should apply this concept with any action you may be taking that is unhealthy: when you have the solution, don't try to do it. Just do it. If you're just "trying" you must still like the pain. If you don't like the pain, something about the process of the self destructive action or inaction you are taking is euphoric to you. So, do what the 'Trumps' of this world tell you, invest and give to the poor. Save money for yourself and your heritage. You CAN do it!

TO ALL MY SISTERS IN THE STRUGGLE

Chapter 11

DON'T LOOK BACK

Sisters, don't look back! I wrote a song a long time before I understood its meaning entitled, "I Won't Fear." A part of the chorus says, "Many things come to hinder us to keep us from achieving our purpose, but I won't fear." Little did I know that this song was purposed for my destiny. So remember the words of this song when you are in trouble. Stay focused no matter what the Enemy throws your way, and don't forget to use those rocks and that dirt as stepping stones! Let me share something with you; during a part of my recovery process, I faced many challenges. The devil would inflict physical pain or health conditions on me. He would put me in remembrance of how much I loved and cared about various men in my past. Later, he would try to tempt me again with suicide and chaos on the job. I recognized the attacks and fought the good fight well. But then, He did something different, right when it had been prophesied to me that I would be receiving blessings, right at the point of my breakthrough, He threw every single weapon in His arsenal at me, at once. Things got so difficult, that I, abruptly, left work one day. I went home, turned up the praise and worship music, and turned on the gospel station; that helped somewhat. Of course, I was praying. The only thing that came out was, "Jesus help me, please help me." I searched my heart and mind for scriptures, but nothing significant came. I began quoting all the scriptures that entered my mind, and then I called my healthy family. Some of them had been experiencing similar setbacks. There was something my sister said that truly saved my mind that day. She said, "Oh, so the Enemy decided to throw everything at you all at once, since, one by one you had fought off all the other attacks." She said, "It's easy to catch one ball... but can you juggle?" Wow! What a revelation that she had unveiled! That did it for me! I was back in the fight! Oh yeah, the mind is definitely the battlefield. Everything happens in the mind. If the Enemy can get you to stop thinking positively, you'll stop acting positively. "Oh yes, Devil, 'check!' It's your move now!" But remember sisters, as in the game of chess, it is best to be three moves ahead of your opponent. So, while you are praising God for the victory, don't forget to be prepared for what the Enemy may do next.

I am quickly learning my areas of temptation, those areas where I notice I always fall victim to attacks like a fly drawn to the splendor of the design of a spider's web. But now, that I know I like shiny designs; I'll pay closer attention to the ones that could be a spider's web (Satan's trap). Know thyself; it will get you through many uphill battles.

My sisters, please note that nothing can be done without God's help, if you haven't noticed from this book, I am a devout believer in Yahweh, who is the God of Abraham, Isaac, and Jacob; the Great I Am. Without God; you can do nothing. I will take this time to express my reason for this belief.

If you have ever wanted to do something or be someone of importance, you had a dream about it. Then, that dream caused you to visualize doing it. As a kid, those dreams may have seemed supernatural, meaning, there is no way that you could do it on this earth, on your own. Whether you admit it now or not, when you were younger, you had dreams and visions of becoming someone great, of doing something unimaginable, something that would make you stand out among your peers, or something that would help you save some aspect of the world you dwell in. Why do you think that was? Now, think about your favorite movies. Think about the idea of someone rescuing someone else, or the idea of that someone being you. Why do you think they are your favorite movies? Do you have the desire to help others around you? Are you concerned when people are hurting or need you to go that extra mile when you're just too exhausted or extended to do more? It's because you were made that way. You were made to be great. You have a *Holy Spirit*; a Supernatural Supreme Being living inside of you that was put there by your Creator, Yahweh. Whenever your spirit hears a conversation or sees something on TV that is supposed to be manifested in you, the *Spirit* responds. You may have experienced the *Spirit* in this situation before but not known what it was. It is that feeling in the pit of your stomach that rises to your eyes and ears until they are both wide-open and alert, in that moment, you'll receive the strategies and vision to express your calling and destiny.

Think about the movies that I'd mentioned earlier and other films of this nature that bring a desire to move and shake. In order to accurately and positively move and shake, you have to become one with the Creator who designed you to bring about change. Think about karate classes; you are participating to learn moves to defend yourself and ways to capture your opponent or enemy. Hear me when I explain this to you, this is real. God is real! And you know He is real whether you want to admit it out loud or not.

Just the thought of having only yourself to turn to when things go wrong is quite frightening. There must be someone bigger and better, not because you are weak necessarily, (which, if you were honest with yourself you would agree that in some areas you are) but because you have endless challenges to face and conquer. Admittedly, some are greater than what your human mind can envision. You might have desires to be seen as a great person or one who is able to conquer the world. Why is that? Again, I will tell you why. Because the Creator, Yahweh, made you for such a time as this. You were built to lead, to succeed. But no man is an island. You have to seek the Creator for super-natural strength to accomplish your destiny. This truth-in-action is enough to keep you focused on becoming a bigger, better, happier, and healthier you.

Now, the decision is yours. You have to choose to believe to trust God, and allow Him to control or assist you in your destiny; however, it would be in your best interest to accept this truth and His help. It may be hard to understand and accept, at first, but like in *The Matrix*, your brain has been wrongly wired so long, until it has scarcely been given the opportunity to truly think Godly thoughts. This Kingdom of Darkness here on earth has you all screwed up and bound! Sisters, that's why you fell for the lies of the men in the first place!

I have shared the truth as best as I know how to you. Now, what are you going to do about it? Again... Getting out of bondage is a process. You are working on it, but it may not be completed, immediately. When I began healing, I would get discouraged if I didn't see immediate results. I wanted to give up. Of course, that would not have helped the situation. It would still have to be resolved one day. I might as well work on it now.

Now, God has given me the opportunity to not fight alone; I had sisters to help me. That was a good feeling. However, I also know from experience that sometimes I may have to fight alone. But I am not really alone, because I have Jesus as my friend and Savior who has told me that God is always with Him and me. He was able to keep working towards His destiny when things really got tough. With Him as an example, I can say like Yolanda Adams in one of her songs, "But still, I rise." There is no use in giving up on life because there is a light at the end of the tunnel. Sometimes you have to climb up a steep slope of rocks to get out of a hole; it's worth the effort. And if you reminisce about where you came from to where you are now, that should make you run or even leap up the steps. So, come on Joshua Generation! You are the new leaders! Just as God instructed Moses to allow Joshua, a brave warrior and man with faith in God, to succeed him as leader of the

Israelites when he died, you are also instructed to succeed the men and women of God who led the way before you. Let God put some super on your natural; it won't hurt, not even a little. After the bandage has been off your wound for a season, the wound is healed and scab-free. Walk with Jesus and with time, you may not even notice where the injury had been. Get healed and be free!

TO ALL MY SISTERS IN THE STRUGGLE

Works Cited

www.christianword.org

Encarta. (1998-2004). *World English Dictionary.* Microsoft Corporation.

H. Paul Stanley Jr., P. (2001). *www.depression-help-for-you.com/self-help-depression.html.* Retrieved November 15, 2008, from www.depression-help-for-you.com: http://www.depression-help-for-you.com/

Wakeshider-Cruse, S., WestCott, C., & Bradshaw, J. Inner Child Guided Imagery.

Other Information

Domestic Violence Hotline
1-800-799-SAFE
Suicide Hotline
1-800-Suicide

Scripture References

http://www.biblegateway.com
Matthew 11:12- King James Version
Psalm 105:14-16- New King James Version
1 Corinthians 10:13- The Message
Romans 8:28- King James Version
Proverbs 4:23-27- The Message
2 Corinthians 10:3-4- The Message
John 16:13- New Living Translation
Romans 7:14-25- New King James Version
Matthew 6:33- King James Version
Nehemiah 8:10- New King James Version
Isaiah 61:3- New King James Version
John 8:32- King James Version
1 Peter 4:12-13- New King James Version
Hebrews 12:1-3- New King James Version
Matthew 25:14-29- New King James Version

TO ALL MY SISTERS IN THE STRUGGLE

ABOUT THE AUTHOR

Natalie M. Lewis is a songstress and orator, the youngest of four girls, a teacher at The Way of Truth Deliverance Institutional Church in Memphis, TN, holds a B.S. in Management Information Systems from Oral Roberts University, is world traveled from Memphis, TN to as far as the Czech Republic, and refers to herself as a "Catalyst" because she wants to make or bring about an immediate and positive change in the lives of women who are seeking hope for a better way of life. This Catalyst has a mandate on her life to nurture and help the hurting or damaged hearts in a speedy effective way without them becoming harmed during the process. Having faced many obstacles, she desires that every child, teen, and young adult realize that with the guidance of God they can overcome any difficulty.

What is her purpose for writing this book? This optimistic author seeks to inform others that there is a light at the end of the tunnel and to guide them to that place in their mind where there is hope; that things will change if they are willing to make the needed sacrifices and acknowledge the help when it arrives.

To contact Natalie or to place orders please visit one of her websites:

- **www.nataliemlewis.com**
- **www.amazon.com**
  Keyword: To All My Sisters in the Struggle

Additional Resources:

To All My Sisters in the Struggle Workbook

TO ALL MY SISTERS IN THE STRUGGLE

www.ingramcontent.com/pod-product-compliance
Ingram Content Group UK Ltd.
Pitfield, Milton Keynes, MK11 3LW, UK
UKHW041958230426
12048UKWH00008B/408